ENGLISH/SPANISH EDITION

The Oxford Picture Dictionary

for Kids

Joan Ross Keyes

Illustrated by Sally Springer

OXFORD UNIVERSITY PRESS

OXFORD
UNIVERSITY PRESS

198 Madison Avenue
New York, NY 10016 USA

Great Clarendon Street
Oxford OX2 6DP England

Oxford New York

Auckland Cape Town Dar es Salaam Hong Kong Karachi
Kuala Lumpur Madrid Melbourne Mexico City Nairobi
New Delhi Shanghai Taipei Toronto

With offices in

Argentina Austria Brazil Chile Czech Republic France Greece
Guatemala Hungary Italy Japan Poland Portugal Singapore
South Korea Switzerland Thailand Turkey Ukraine Vietnam

OXFORD is a trademark of Oxford University Press.

ISBN: 978 0 19 436662 5

Editorial Manager: Shelagh Speers
Senior Editor: June Schwartz
Editor: Dorothy Bukantz
Production Editor: M. Long
Elementary Design Manager: Doris Chen
Designer: David Hildebrand
Art Buyer: Donna Goldberg
Production Manager: Abram Hall
Production Controller: Georgiann Baran

Printing (last digit): 10

Printed in China.

Translation and Production by Editorial options, inc.
Cover illustration by Sally Springer
Illustrations by Sally Springer
Cover design by Doris Chen

Additional art by: Gary Torrisi; Robert Frank/Melissa Turk & The Artist
Network; Marcia Hartsock, CMI; Elizabeth Wolf/Melissa Turk & The Artist
Network; Andrea Tachiera; Stephen Nicodemus; and John Paul Genzo.

This book is printed on paper from certified and well-managed sources.

Acknowledgements

To all my students everywhere whose appreciation and enthusiasm motivated me to create this book, its stories, dialogues,
and Beats!

To the special people at Oxford University Press: the design and production staff for ingeniously putting all the parts together, to
Shelagh Speers, the Editorial Manager, for her "go for it" encouragement, and most of all to my own editor, June Schwartz, whose
patient labors got us through it all.

And to my family, my daughter and three sons, for understanding and giving me space...

I thank you all.

JRK

The Oxford Picture Dictionary for Kids is designed especially for young students, ages five to seven, who are learning English.

The dictionary presents over 700 words in the context of pictures that tell stories. Five characters and their families are introduced at the beginning of the book, and appear throughout in 60 double-page illustrations.

Dictionary Organization

Each double-page illustration introduces a topic. The 60 topics are organized into nine themes. The initial focus is on the individual characters' experiences within the family, at home, and at school. The focus then expands to include their experiences in the neighborhood, around the town, and in other environments in the United States and around the world. Although the topics follow a logical progression, each topic is self-contained so that they may be presented to students in any order.

Under the double-page illustration in each topic are words and pictures corresponding to the objects or actions shown in that illustration. Each word is accompanied by a small picture that duplicates the item in the larger illustration. These *callouts* define the words. They help children isolate each item and search for it in the context of the picture story.

Each topic has 12 numbered callouts. In addition to the callout vocabulary, some pages have labels, such as for rooms in the house and in the school. The number of words has been kept to a minimum so that students will be able to master the vocabulary more easily. Verbs and nouns are included in topics together to encourage students to use the language in

context. Verbs are grouped together on the page. Each verb is marked with a star.

Appendix and Word Lists

Following the 60 topics is an appendix that includes the alphabet, numbers, colors, shapes, days, months, and time.

After the appendix are three lists: *Words, Verbs,* and *Subjects.* The *Words* list, arranged alphabetically, includes the callout nouns and verbs, labels, and key words from the titles. These are listed in black. Listed in red are additional words that do not appear in the text, but are pictured in the illustrations.

The *Verbs* list is arranged by the topics in which verbs can be found.

The *Subjects* list is a convenient cross-reference, by category, of words that can be found within several different topics and themes.

Using the Dictionary as a Program

The dictionary can be used by itself or with other components that make it suitable as the core of an entire English-language curriculum. These components include the *Teacher's Book, Reproducibles Collection, Workbook, Cassettes,* and *Wall Charts.*

The Reproducibles Collection is a boxed set of four books of reproducible pages: *Word and Picture Cards, Stories, Beats!,* and *Worksheets.* The *Stories* describe each illustration; the *Beats!* are playful rhythmic chants for each topic. In the *Stories* and *Beats!* books, each illustrated sheet folds to make a mini-book for students to take home.

The *Teacher's Book,* in addition to complete notes for every topic, contains annotated bibliographies of appropriate theme-related literature to help create a classroom library.

The *Picture Dictionary* is available in both monolingual and bilingual editions.

Prefacio

The Oxford Picture Dictionary for Kids
(Diccionario Infantil Ilustrado Oxford) ha sido
especialmente creado para estudiantes de cinco a
siete años que están aprendiendo inglés. El
diccionario contiene más de 700 palabras agrupadas
en una serie de dibujos que cuentan historias. Al
principio del libro se presentan a cinco personajes y
sus familias, los cuales aparecen a lo largo de las 60
ilustraciones del libro.

Organización del diccionario

Cada ilustración presenta una escena. Las 60
escenas están organizadas en nueve temas. El libro
está enfocado inicialmente en las experiencias de
los personajes y su interacción en la familia, el
hogar y la escuela. Más adelante, el enfoque se
amplía para incluir las experiencias de estos
personajes en el barrio, la ciudad y otros ambientes
de Estados Unidos y del mundo. A pesar de que las
escenas siguen un orden lógico, cada una de ellas
es totalmente independiente de las otras, por lo que
pueden ser presentadas a los estudiantes sin seguir
un orden determinado.

Bajo las ilustraciones a doble página de cada
escena, se encuentran palabras y dibujos que
corresponden a los objetos o las acciones que se
muestran en dicha ilustración. Cada palabra está
acompañada de un dibujo pequeño que reproduce
un detalle de la escena. Estos dibujos definen las
palabras, ayudan a los niños a aislar cada cosa y a
buscarla en el contexto del cuento gráfico.

Cada escena tiene 12 entradas numeradas. Además
del vocabulario de los dibujos, algunas páginas
tienen rótulos, como, por ejemplo, los que aparecen
en las habitaciones de una casa o los salones de una
escuela. Se ha incluido un número mínimo de
palabras para que los estudiantes puedan dominar
el vocabulario más fácilmente. Los verbos y los
sustantivos se incluyen juntos para animar a los

estudiantes a usar el idioma en contexto. Los verbos
se agrupan juntos en la página. Cada verbo está
señalado con una estrella.

Apéndice y Listas de palabras

Al final de las 60 escenas hay un apéndice que
incluye el alfabeto, los números, los colores, las
formas geométricas, los días, los meses y la hora.

Después del apéndice hay tres listas: *Palabras*,
Verbos y *Materias*. La lista de *Palabras*, que está en
orden alfabético, incluye las entradas de los
sustantivos y verbos, rótulos y palabras clave de
los títulos. Esta lista aparece en tinta negra. En tinta
roja se señalan palabras adicionales que no
aparecen en el texto, pero que se muestran en
las ilustraciones.

La lista de *Verbos* muestra en orden los temas en
donde aparecen verbos.

La lista de *Materias* es una referencia útil de palabras
clasificadas de acuerdo a varios temas y materias.

Uso del diccionario como programa de enseñanza

Este diccionario se puede usar solo o junto con
otros componentes, lo que lo hace apropiado como
el núcleo de un currículo completo para el estudio
del idioma inglés. Estos componentes incluyen la
Guía del maestro, *Materiales reproducibles*, el *Cuaderno
de trabajo*, *Casetes* y las *Láminas grandes*.

Los *Materiales reproducibles* se ofrecen en una caja
que contiene cuatro libros de hojas reproducibles:
Tarjetas de palabras y dibujos, *Cuentos*, *¡Ritmo!* y *Hojas
de trabajo*. Los *Cuentos* describen cada ilustración.
¡Ritmo! son alegres cantos rítmicos para cada
materia. Cada hoja ilustrada de los *Cuentos* y el
libro *¡Ritmo!* se puede doblar para crear un
minilibro que los estudiantes pueden llevar a
sus casas.

La *Guía del maestro*, además de contener
anotaciones completas para cada materia, contiene
bibliografía de obras literarias apropiadas y de
alguna forma relacionadas con los temas, que se
sugieren para ayudar a crear una biblioteca del
salón de clase.

El *Diccionario Ilustrado* se encuentra disponible en
ediciones bilingües y monolingües.

Contents

Theme 4: My Town (All Around) / Mi ciudad

Me

Yo

Ting

Tommy

Alison

Zoe

Diego

My family

Mi familia

The Matthews family
La familia Matthews

The Cheng family
La familia Cheng

The Young family
La familia Young

1. sister
   hermana

2. brother
   hermano

3. mother
   madre

4. father
   padre

5. parents
   padres

6.  children
   hijos

The Lopez family
La familia Lopez

The Jackson family
La familia Jackson

7. grandmother
abuela

8. grandfather
abuelo

9. aunt
tía

10. uncle
tío

11. cousins
primos

12. baby
bebé

Different faces
Caras diferentes

1. eyes
   ojos

2. ears
   orejas

3. nose
   nariz

4. mouth
   boca

5. tooth / teeth
   dientes

6. chin
   barbilla

7. **eyelashes**
pestañas

8. **skin**
piel

9. **hair**
pelo

10. **straight**
lacio

11. **curly**
rizado

12. **glasses**
anteojos

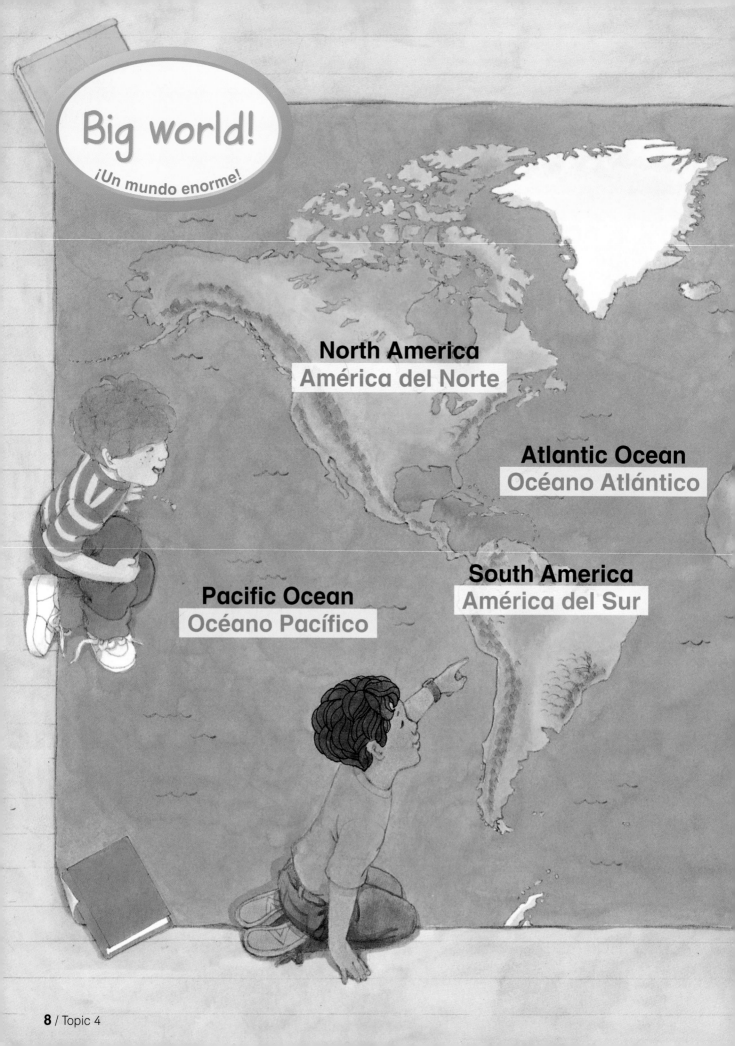

Big world!

¡Un mundo enorme!

North America
América del Norte

Atlantic Ocean
Océano Atlántico

South America
América del Sur

Pacific Ocean
Océano Pacífico

Europe
Europa

Asia
Asia

Africa
África

Australia
Australia

Antarctica
Antártida

Where do you live?

¿Dónde víves?

1. **house**
casa

2. **apartment**
departamento

3. **hill**
colina

4. **street**
calle

5. **address**
dirección

6. **telephone**
teléfono

7.		**window** ventana	10.		**tree** árbol
8.		**door** puerta	11.		**yard** patio
9.		**roof** techo	12.		**fence** cerca

bedroom dormitorio

Good morning!
¡Buenos días!

bathroom

living room sala

1. stove
   estufa

2. table
   mesa

3. sink
   fregadero

4. dresser
   tocador

5. bed
   cama

6. sofa
   sofá

baño

bedroom dormitorio

kitchen cocina

 7. cook
cocinar

 8. eat
comer

9. wash
lavar

10. brush
cepillar

11. get dressed
vestirse

12. sleep
dormir

Busy bathroom!

¡Baño ocupado!

1. water
   agua

2. brush
   cepillo

3. comb
   peine

4. bathtub
   bañera

5. shower
   ducha

6. toothbrush
   cepillo de dientes

7. **toothpaste**
pasta de dientes

8. **shampoo**
champú

9. **soap**
jabón

10. **towel**
toalla

11. **toilet**
inodoro

12. **toilet paper**
papel higiénico

What can I wear?
¿Qué me pongo?

1. **sweater**
suéter

2. **underwear**
ropa interior

3. **sneakers**
zapatos tenis

4. **socks**
calcetines

5. **baseball cap**
gorra de béisbol

6. **dress**
vestido

 7. skirt
falda

 10. T-shirt
camiseta

 8. sweatshirt
sudadera

 11. boots
botas

 9. jeans
pantalones de mezclilla

 12. pajamas
pijama

Who made breakfast?
¿Quién hizo el desayuno?

1.  bowl
   tazón

2. plate
   plato

3. cup
   taza

4. glass
   vaso

5. knife
   cuchillo

6. fork
   tenedor

7. **spoon**
cuchara

8. **juice**
jugo

9. **butter**
mantequilla

10. **cereal**
cereal

11. **eggs**
huevos

12. **bread**
pan

1. **bus stop**
   parada de autobús

2. **bus driver**
   conductor de autobús

3. **corner**
   esquina

4. **line**
   fila

5. **seat**
   asiento

6. **seat belt**
   cinturón de seguridad

7.		**lunch box** lonchera	☆10.		**push** empujar

7. **lunch box**
lonchera

☆10. **push**
empujar

8. **backpack**
mochila

☆11. **stand**
pararse

☆9. **lean**
recostarse

☆12. **sit**
sentarse

Time for school
En la escuela

classroom
salón de clase

office
oficina

1. teacher
   maestro(a)

2. principal
   director(a)

3. nurse
   enfermero(a)

4. student
   estudiante

5. crossing guard
   guardia escolar

6. librarian
   bibliotecario(a)

brary
lioteca

art room
salón de arte

music room
salón de música

urse's office
enfermería

cafeteria
cafetería

gym
gimnasio

7. car
   automóvil

8. bicycle
   bicicleta

9. bus
   autobús

10. clock
    reloj

☆11.  walk
    caminar

☆12.  ride
    montar

What are
you making?

¿Qué haces?

Mrs. Diaz

1. **picture**
   dibujo

2. **markers**
   marcadores

3. **pencil**
   lápiz

4. **crayons**
   creyones

5. **scissors**
   tijeras

6. **glue**
   pegamento

7. **blocks**
bloques

☆8. **build**
construir

☆9. **listen**
escuchar

☆10.  **look**
mirar

☆11. **paint**
pintar

☆12. **cut**
cortar

Where's my homework?
¿Dónde está mi tarea?

Homework
Write a story.
Draw a picture.

1. book
libro

2. notebook
libreta

3. paper
papel

4. board
pizarrón

5. desk
escritorio

6. chair
silla

7.   **chalk**
    tiza

8.   **wastebasket**
    cesto de papeles

☆9.  **write**
    escribir

☆10. **draw**
     dibujar

☆11. **read**
     leer

☆12. **think**
     pensar

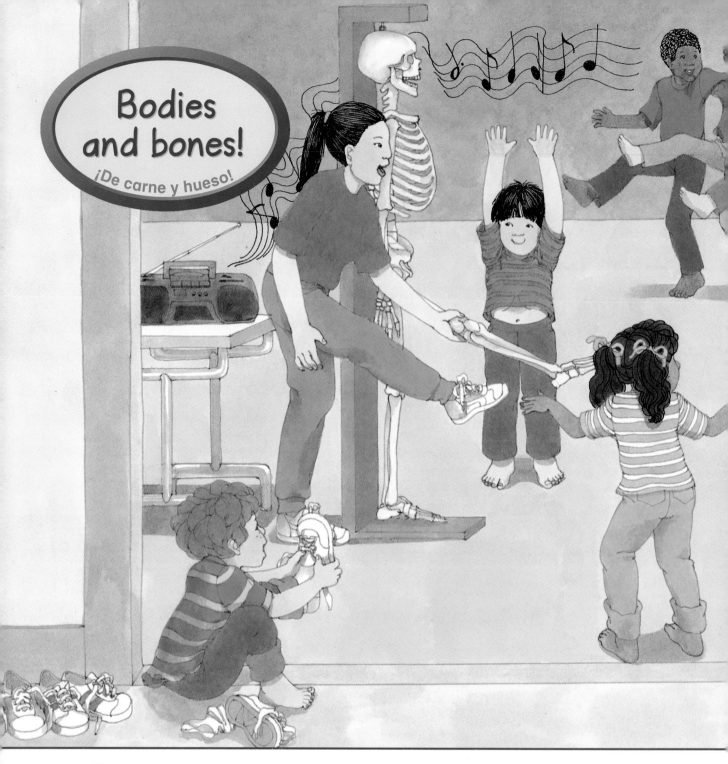

Bodies and bones!
¡De carne y hueso!

1. **head**
   cabeza

2. **neck**
   cuello

3. **chest**
   pecho

4. **stomach**
   estómago

5. **back**
   espalda

6. **buttocks**
   glúteos

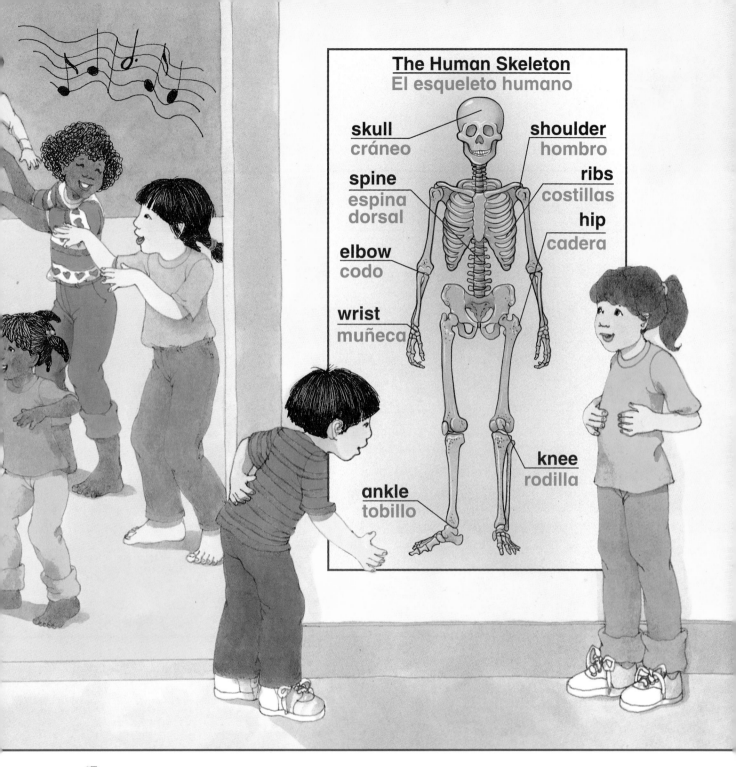

The Human Skeleton
El esqueleto humano

skull
cráneo

shoulder
hombro

spine
espina dorsal

ribs
costillas

hip
cadera

elbow
codo

wrist
muñeca

knee
rodilla

ankle
tobillo

7. leg
pierna

10. arm
brazo

8. foot / feet
pie

11. hand
mano

9. toes
dedos de los pies

12. fingers
dedos

1. **happy**
   alegre

2. **sad**
   triste

3. **tired**
   cansado

4. **surprised**
   sorprendido

5. **angry**
   enojado

6. **scared**
   asustado

7. **worried**
preocupado

☆10. **cry**
llorar

☆8. **smile**
sonreír

☆11. **frown**
fruncir el ceño

☆9. **yawn**
bostezar

☆12. **laugh**
reír

Gym time!

¡Hora de gimnasia!

1. **hoop**
aro

2. **around**
alrededor

3. **between**
entre

4. **over**
sobre

5. **through**
a través

6. **under**
debajo

7. **mat**
   tapete

☆8. **skip**
   brincar

☆9. **hop**
   saltar

☆10. **crawl**
   arrastrarse

☆11. **jump**
   brincar

☆12. **tumble**
   rodar

What's for lunch?
¿Qué hay de almuerzo?

1. **tray**
   bandeja

2. **taco**
   taco

3. **apple**
   manzana

4. **milk**
   leche

5. **can**
   lata

6. **carrot**
   zanahoria

7. **egg roll**
rollo

8. **sushi**
sushi

9. **garbage can**
bote de basura

10. **sandwich**
sándwich

11. **salad**
ensalada

12. **cookie**
galleta dulce

Let's play!

¡A jugar!

1. **swing**
   columpio

2. **slide**
   resbaladilla

3. **bars**
   barras

4. **seesaw**
   subibaja

5. **ball**
   pelota

☆6. **climb**
   trepar

 7. **throw**
lanzar

 8. **catch**
agarrar

 9. **bounce**
botar

 10. **fall**
caer

 11. **run**
correr

 12. **kick**
patear

What's the matter?

¿Qué te pasa?

1. **stomachache**
   dolor de estómago

2. **tissues**
   pañuelos desechables

3. **sore throat**
   dolor de garganta

4. **fever**
   fiebre

5. **thermometer**
   termómetro

6. **bandage**
   vendaje

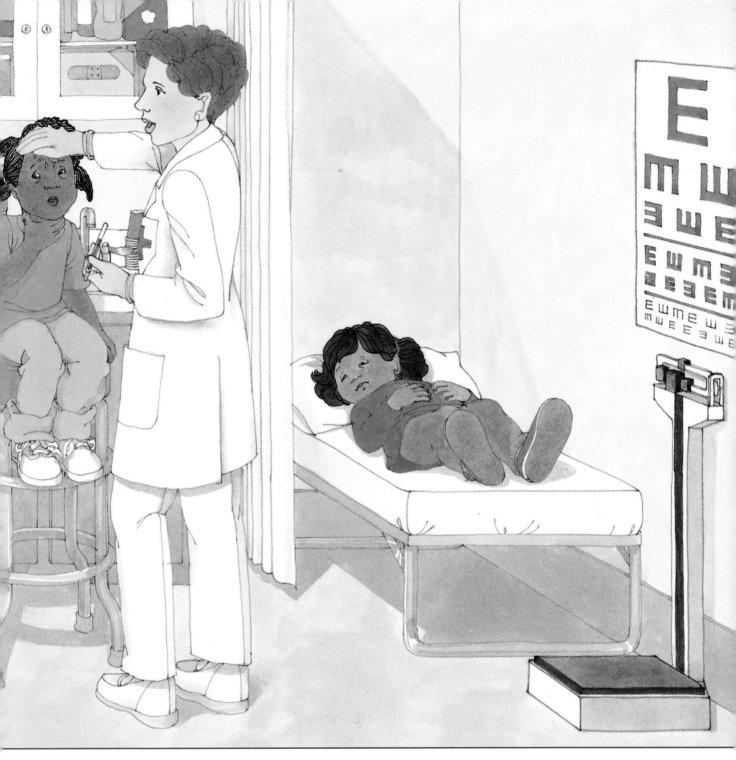

7. **blood**
sangre

8.  **cut**
cortadura

9. **bump**
chichón

☆10. **cough**
toser

☆11. **sneeze**
estornudar

☆12. **lie down**
acostarse

Music!

¡Música!

1. violin
   violín

2. trumpet
   trompeta

3. tuba
   tuba

4. flute
   flauta

5. maracas
   maracas

6. piano
   piano

7. **bongo drums**
bongó

8. **triangle**
triángulo

9. **blow**
soplar

*10. **beat**
marcar el compás

*11. **clap**
dar palmadas

*12. **sing**
cantar

1. police officer
   policía

2. traffic
   tráfico

3. traffic light
   semáforo

4. truck
   camión

5. motorcycle
   motocicleta

6.  taxi
   taxi

7.		**police station** estación de policía	10.	**pet shop** tienda de mascotas
8.		**library** biblioteca	11. 	**barbershop** barbería
9.		**sports store** tienda de deportes	12. 	**toy store** tienda de juguetes

Look at the toys!
¡Mira los juguetes!

1. **game**
juego

2. **airplane**
avión

3. **boat**
bote

4. **doll**
muñeca

5. **animals**
animales

6. **train**
tren

7. **money**
dinero

8. **quarter**
moneda de 25¢

9. **dime**
moneda de 10¢

10. **nickel**
moneda de 5¢

11. **penny**
centavo

12. **dollar**
dólar

Can we have a pet?

¿Podemos tener una mascota?

1. **bird**
pájaro

2. **fish**
pez

3. **fish tank**
pecera

4. **turtle**
tortuga

5. **mouse**
ratón

6. **cage**
jaula

7. dog
   perro

8. cat
   gato

9. kitten
   gatito

10. puppy
    perrito

11. collar
    collar

12. leash
    correa

Let's go to the library!

¡Vamos a la biblioteca!

AUTHOR: KEYES, J.R.
TITLE: OUR EARTH
SUBJECT: EARTH SCIENCE
CALL NUMBER: 551 K

1. magazine
   revista

2. newspaper
   periódico

3.  atlas
   atlas

4. dictionary
   diccionario

5. computer
   computadora

6. call number
   número de catálogo

7.	**videotape** videocasete	10.	**due date** fecha de vencimiento
8. 	**bookshelves** estantes	☆11.	**check out** registrar
9. 	**library card** tarjeta de biblioteca	☆12.	**return** devolver

I'm sick!

¡Estoy enfermo!

examination room
sala de reconocimiento

1. doctor
doctor(a)

2. patient
paciente

3. checkup
examen

4. chart
récord médico

5. scale
balanza

6. stethoscope
estetoscopio

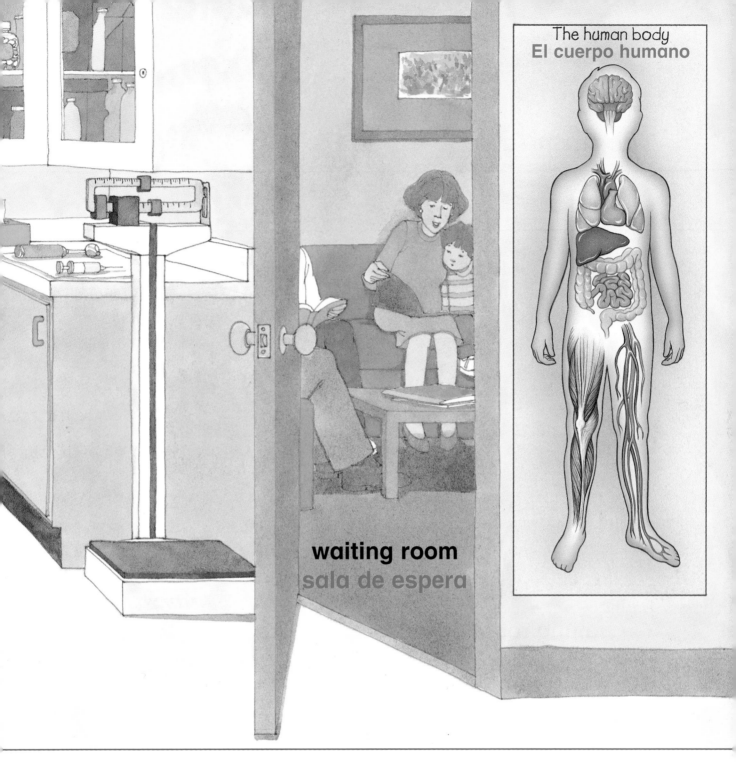

The human body
El cuerpo humano

waiting room
sala de espera

7. **medicine**
medicina

8. **drops**
gotas

9. **spray**
aerosol

10. **prescription**
receta

11. **tablets**
tabletas

12. **shot**
inyección

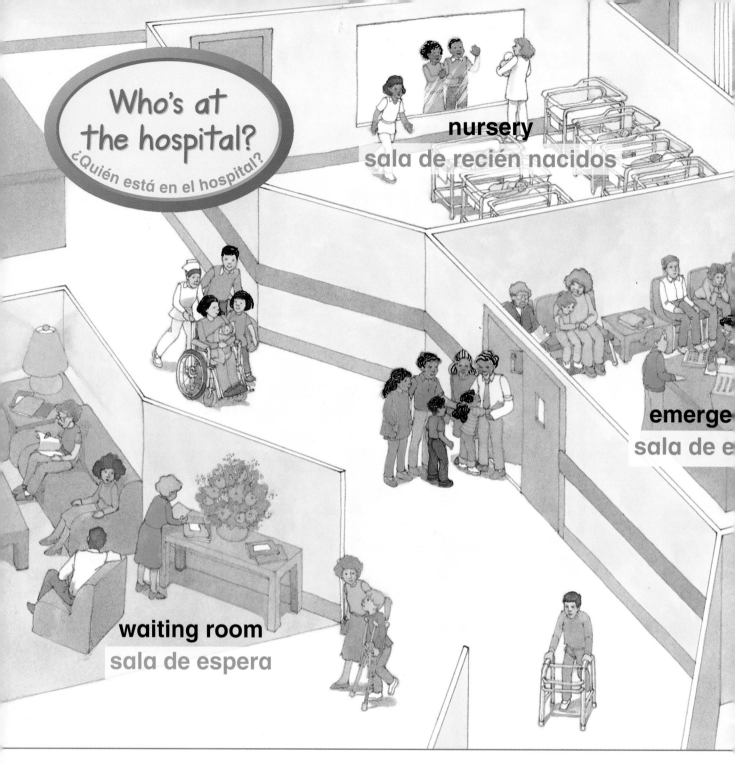

Who's at the hospital?
¿Quién está en el hospital?

nursery
sala de recién nacidos

waiting room
sala de espera

emerge
sala de e

1.  siren
   sirena

2.  ambulance
   ambulancia

3.  paramedic
   paramédico(a)

4. stretcher
   camilla

5. mask
   máscara

6. rubber gloves
   guantes de goma

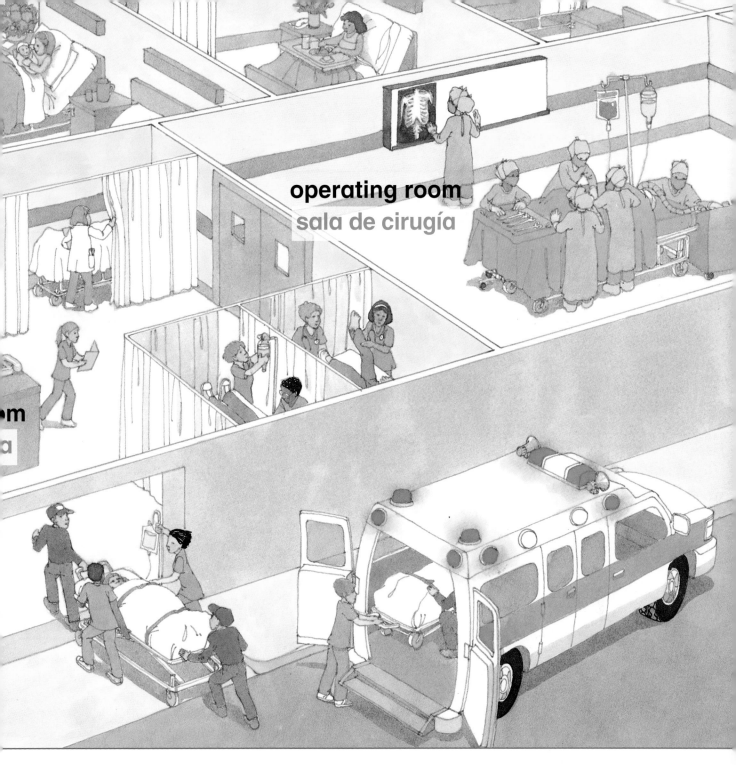

operating room
sala de cirugía

7.		**X ray** radiografía	10.		**crutches** muletas
8.		**wheelchair** silla de ruedas	11.		**cast** yeso
9.		**walker** andador	12.		**blanket** manta

Busy supermarket!

¡Supermercado movido!

1. list
   lista

2. pineapple
   piña

3. bananas
   plátanos

4. orange
   naranja

5. meat
   carne

6.  seafood
   mariscos

7.	**box** caja	10.	**lettuce** lechuga
8.	**bags** bolsas	11.	**broccoli** brócoli
9.	**cart** carrito de compras	12.	**cheese** queso

Errands in town
Mandados

1. restaurant
   restaurante

2. hardware store
   ferretería

3. drugstore
   farmacia

4. letter
   carta

5. letter carrier
   cartero(a)

6. mailbox
   buzón

7.		**post office** oficina de correos	10.	**bakery** panadería
8.		**dentist** dentista	11.	**bank** banco
9.		**laundry** lavandería	12.	**gas station** gasolinera

7. **post office** oficina de correos

8. **dentist** dentista

9. **laundry** lavandería

10. **bakery** panadería

11. **bank** banco

12. **gas station** gasolinera

Dinner's ready!
¡La cena está lista!

1. **roast beef**
   carne de res asada

2. **potato**
   papa

3. **peas**
   chícharos

4.  **tomato**
   tomate

5.  **rolls**
   rollos

6. **apple pie**
   pastel de manzana

7. soup
sopa

8. corn
maíz

9. chicken
pollo

10. rice
arroz

11. beans
frijoles

12. melon
melón

Nice evening!

¡Linda tarde!

1. **stereo**
   estéreo

2. **television**
   televisor

3.  **remote**
   control remoto

4. **CD**
   disco compacto

5. **headphones**
   audífonos

6. **radio**
   radio

7. **rest**
descansar

8.  **play**
jugar

9. **watch**
mirar

10. **help**
ayudar

11. **talk**
hablar

12. **practice**
practicar

Saturday at the mall

Un sábado de compras

1. **movie theater**
cine

2. **arcade**
salón de juegos

3. **snack bar**
merendero

4. **pizza**
pizza

5. **french fries**
papas fritas

6. **ice cream cone**
barquillo

7. soda
   refresco

8.  shoe store
   zapatería

9.  clothing store
   tienda de ropa

10. rest rooms
    baños

11. escalator
    escalera eléctrica

12. exit
    salida

1. balloon
   globo

2. present
   regalo

3. card
   tarjeta

4. ribbon
   cinta

5. wrapping paper
   papel de envolver

6. baseball bat
   bate de béisbol

January	February
S M T W T F S	S M T W T F S
1	1 2 3 4 5
2 3 4 5 6 7 8	6 7 8 9 10 11 12
9 10 11 12 13 14 15	13 14 15 16 17 18 19
16 17 18 19 20 21 22	20 21 22 23 24 25 26
23 24 25 26 27 28 29	27 28
30 31	

March	April
S M T W T F S	S M T W T F S
1 2 3 4	1
5 6 7 8 9 10 11	2 3 4 5 6 7 8
12 13 14 15 16 17 18	9 10 11 12 13 14 15
19 20 21 22 23 24 25	16 17 18 19 20 21 22
26 27 28 29 30 31	23 24 25 26 27 28 29
	30

May	June
S M T W T F S	S M T W T F S
1 2 3 4 5 6	1 2 3
7 8 9 10 11 12 13	4 5 6 7 8 9 10
14 15 16 17 18 19 20	11 12 13 14 15 16 17
21 22 23 24 25 26 27	18 19 20 21 22 23 24
28 29 30 31	25 26 27 28 29 30

July	August
S M T W T F S	S M T W T F S
1	1 2 3 4 5
2 3 4 5 6 7 8	6 7 8 9 10 11 12
9 10 11 12 13 14 15	13 14 15 16 17 18 19
16 17 18 19 20 21 22	20 21 22 23 24 25 26
23 24 25 26 27 28 29	27 28 29 30 31
30 31	

September	October
S M T W T F S	S M T W T F S
1 2	1 2 3 4 5 6 7
3 4 5 6 7 8 9	8 9 10 11 12 13 14
10 11 12 13 14 15 16	15 16 17 18 19 20 21
17 18 19 20 21 22 23	22 23 24 25 26 27 28
24 25 26 27 28 29 30	29 30 31

November	December
S M T W T F S	S M T W T F S
1 2 3 4	1 2
5 6 7 8 9 10 11	3 4 5 6 7 8 9
12 13 14 15 16 17 18	10 11 12 13 14 15 16
19 20 21 22 23 24 25	17 18 19 20 21 22 23
26 27 28 29 30	24 25 26 27 28 29 30
	31

7. jewelry
joyas

8. puzzle
crucigrama

9. helicopter
helicóptero

10. candy
dulce

11. cake
pastel

12.  candles
velas

Sunday in the city

Un domingo en la ciudad

1. **airport**
   aeropuerto

2.  **railroad**
   ferrocarril

3. **highway**
   autopista

4. **factory**
   fábrica

5. **smokestack**
   chimenea

6. **litter**
   basura

7.		**street cleaner** barrendero(a)	10.		**park** parque
8.		**garbage truck** camión de basura	11.		**bench** banca
9.		**skyscrapers** rascacielos	12.		**subway** metro

Street scene
Escena callejera

1. singer
   cantante

2. dancer
   bailarín(a)

3. musician
   músico(a)

4. guitar
   guitarra

5. photographer
   fotógrafo(a)

6. camera
   cámara

7. theater
teatro

8. museum
museo

9. steps
escalones

10. mime
mimo

11.  artist
artista

12. painting
pintura

New building going up!

¡Edificio en construcción!

DANGER KEEP OUT

DANGER KEEP OUT

1. **backhoe**
excavadora

2. **dump truck**
camión de volteo

3. **cement mixer**
mezcladora de cemento

4. **crane**
grúa

5. **forklift**
montacargas

6. **bulldozer**
niveladora

7.		construction worker albañil	10.		electrician electricista
8.		carpenter carpintero	11.		pipe tubería
9.		plumber plomero	12.		wire alambre

Fire!

¡Fuego!

1. **smoke**
   humo

2. **flame**
   llama

3. **fire engine**
   camión de bomberos

4. **firefighter**
   bombero

5. **fire chief**
   jefe de bomberos

6. **fire hydrant**
   hidrante

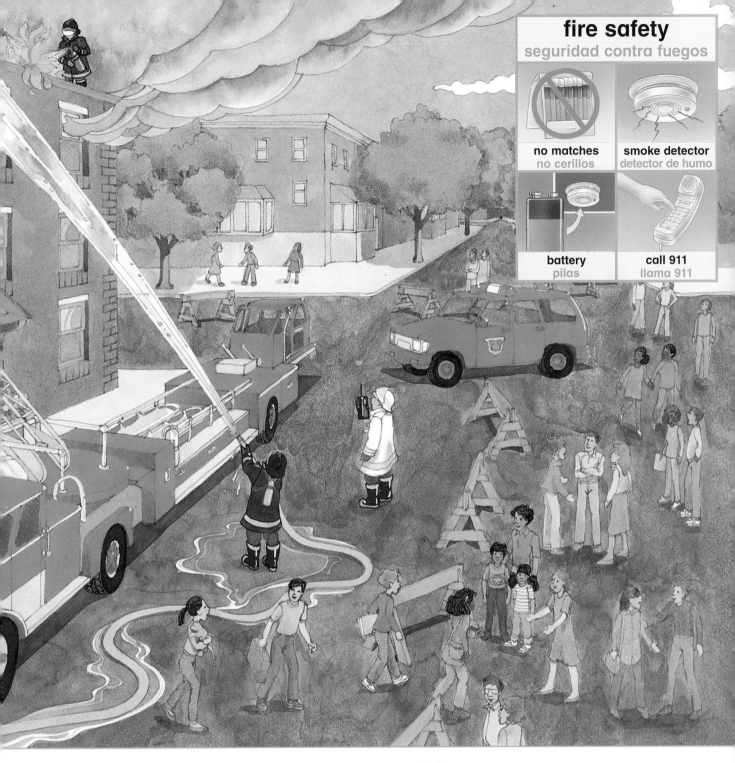

fire safety
seguridad contra fuegos

no matches
no cerillos

smoke detector
detector de humo

battery
pilas

call 911
llama 911

7. 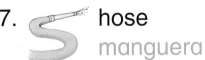 hose
manguera

8. axe
hacha

9. ladder
escalera

10. air tank
tanque de aire

11. fire extinguisher
extinguidor

12. fire escape
escalera de incendios

Big harbor

El gran puerto

1. **sunset**
   puesta de sol

2. **lighthouse**
   faro

3. **ship**
   barco

4. **buoy**
   boya

5. **sailboat**
   velero

6. **bridge**
   puente

7. **ferry**
   transbordador

8. **dock**
   muelle

9. **barge**
   barcaza

10. **warehouse**
    almacén

11. **tugboat**
    remolcador

12. **anchor**
    ancla

Carnival!

¡Carnaval!

1. **ticket**
   boleto

2. **popcorn**
   palomitas de maíz

3. **cotton candy**
   algodón de azúcar

4. **acrobat**
   acróbata

5. **trapeze**
   trapecio

6. **costume**
   disfraz

7. **magician**
mago

8. **clown**
payaso

9. **Ferris wheel**
estrella

10. **carousel**
carrusel

11. **puppet show**
teatro de títeres

12. **fireworks**
fuegos artificiales

Great restaurant!

¡Magnífico restaurante!

1.  **tablecloth**
mantel

2. **napkin**
servilleta

3. **apron**
delantal

4. **pots**
cacerolas

5. **chef**
jefe de cocina

6. **menu**
menú

7.	**chopsticks** palillos chinos	☆10.	**stir** mover
8.	**waiter** mesero(a)	☆11.	**chop** picar
☆9.	**pour** verter	☆12.	**serve** servir

Let's see the USA!

¡Vamos a ver Estados Unidos!

1. **desert**
   desierto

2. **peninsula**
   península

3. **mountains**
   montañas

4. **lake**
   lago

5. **gulf**
   golfo

6. **coast**
   costa

7. forest
   bosque

8. river
   río

9. wetlands
   tierras pantanosas

10. plains
    llanuras

11. glacier
    glaciar

12. island
    isla

Beach day

¡Día de playa!

1. **seagull**
   gaviota

2. **sand**
   arena

3. **wave**
   ola

4. **sunburn**
   quemadura de sol

5. **sunblock**
   protector solar

6.  **lifeguard**
   salvavidas

7.	**surfboard** tabla de surf	☆10.	**swim** nadar
8.	**bathing suit** traje de baño	☆11.	**dive** zambullir
9.	**kite** cometa	☆12.	**float** flotar

We found a tide pool!

¡Encontramos una poza!

BIRD SANCTUARY KEEP OUT

1. pail
cubo

2. shovel
pala

3. stones
piedras

4. shells
conchas

5. clams
almejas

6. crabs
cangrejos

7. snail
   caracol

8. minnows
   pez pequeño

9. seaweed
   alga

10.  duck
    pato

11. goose / geese
    ganso

12. pelican
    pelícano

What's under the sea?

¿Qué hay en el mar?

1.  dolphin
delfín

2. whale
ballena

3. spout
chorro

4. fins
aletas

5. snorkel
esnórquel

6.  school
banco de peces

7. **coral reef**
arrecife de coral

8. **sea horse**
caballito de mar

9. **shark**
tiburón

10. **jellyfish**
medusa

11. **octopus**
pulpo

12. **tentacles**
tentáculos

Working on the farm
En la granja

1. farmer
   granjero

2. barn
   granero

3. tractor
   tractor

4. cow
   vaca

5. hen
   gallina

6.  rooster
   gallo

7. sheep
oveja

8. pig
cerdo

☆9. drive
manejar

☆10. pick
recoger

☆11. feed
alimentar

☆12. milk
ordeñar

Camping out
Acampar

1. **sunrise**
   amanecer

2. **waterfall**
   cascada

3. **tent**
   tienda

4. **sleeping bag**
   saco de dormir

5. **life jacket**
   chaleco salvavidas

6. **rowboat**
   bote de remos

7.	**fishing rod** caña de pescar	10.	 **deer** ciervo
8.	**poison ivy** hiedra venenosa	11.	**bear** oso
9.	**frog** rana	12.	**woods** bosque

Bugs!

¡Insectos!

larva
larva

eggs
huevos

pupa
pupa

adult adulto

1. ant
   hormiga

2. spider
   araña

3. web
   telaraña

4. caterpillar
   oruga

5. cocoon
   capullo

6. butterfly
   mariposa

7. bee
   abeja

8. ticks
   garrapata

9. firefly
   luciérnaga

10. mosquito
    mosquito

11. magnifying glass
    lupa

12. bug spray
    repelente de insectos

Ranch in
the desert

Rancho en el desierto

1. **cowhand**
vaquero

2. **cactus**
cacto

3. **rattlesnake**
serpiente de cascabel

4. **coyote**
coyote

5. **prairie dog**
marmota de las prader

6.  **lizard**
lagartija

7. **horseback riding**
montar a caballo

8. **rocks**
rocas

9. **lasso**
lazo

10. **buffalo**
bisonte

11. **scorpion**
alacrán

12. **horse**
caballo

Dinosaur days

La época de los dinosaurios

1. **fossil**
fósil

2. **scientist**
científico

3.  **dinosaurs**
dinosaurios

4. **Oviraptor**
oviráptor

5. **Pterosaur**
pterosaurio

6. **Triceratops**
triceratops

7. Stegosaurus
estegosaurio

8. Tyrannosaurus Rex
tiranosaurio rex

9. Diplodocus
diplodocus

10. asteroid
asteroide

11. volcano
volcán

12. lava
lava

Who lives in the zoo?

¿Quién vive en la zoológico?

AUSTRALIAN ANIMALS

ASIAN ANIMALS

1. **peacock**
pavo real

2. **monkeys**
monos

3. **elephant**
elefante

4. **tiger**
tigre

5. **lion**
león

6. **snakes**
culebras

7. ape
simios

8. feathers
plumas

9. tail
rabo

10. trunk
trompa

11. scales
escamas

12. fur
piel

I'm in Australia!

¡Estoy en Australia!

1. emu
emú

2. dingo
dingo

3. koala
koala

4. kangaroo
canguro

5. joey
canguro joven

6. wichity grubs
larvas

7. **wombat** oso australiano	10. **claws** garras
8. **kookaburra** martín cazador	11. **pouch** bolsa
9. **parrot** cotorra	12. **wings** alas

I'm in
Africa!

¡Estoy en África!

1. gazelle
   gacela

2. hippopotamus
   hipopótamo

3. zebra
   cebra

4. giraffe
   jirafa

5. gorilla
   gorila

6. chimpanzee
   chimpancé

7. baboon
   mandril

8. flamingo
   flamenco

9. leopard
   leopardo

10. jaws
    mandíbulas

11. spots
    manchas

12. stripes
    franjas

I'm in Asia!

¡Estoy en Asia!

1. **camel**
   camello

2. **orangutan**
   orangután

3. **crocodile**
   cocodrilo

4. **cobra**
   cobra

5. **rhinoceros**
   rinoceronte

6. **egret**
   garza

7. **panda**
panda

8. **bamboo**
bambú

9. **humps**
jorobas

10. **horn**
cuerno

11. **beak**
pico

12. **fangs**
colmillos

Spring is here!
¡Llegó la primavera!

1. **grass**
hierba

2. **bush**
maleza

3. **flowers**
flores

4. **lawn mower**
podadora

5. **rabbit**
conejo

6. **seeds**
semillas

dig	plant	cover	water
cavar	sembrar	cubrir	regar

7. robin
   petirrojo

8. nest
   nido

9. squirrel
   ardilla

10. raccoon
    mapache

11. hammer
    martillo

12. saw
    serrucho

We planted a garden!

¡Hicimos un jardín!

Our Garden

1. **sunshine**
luz solar

2. **rain**
lluvia

3. **soil**
tierra

4. **seed**
semilla

5. **root**
raíz

6. **sprout**
brote

7. **stem**
   tallo

8. **leaf**
   hoja

9. **bud**
   cogollo

10. **flower**
    flor

11. **raincoat**
    impermeable

12. **umbrella**
    sombrilla

Hot summer

Verano caliente

1. **pool**
   alberca

2.  **baseball**
   béisbol

3.  **tennis**
   tenis

4. **waterskiing**
   esquí acuático

5.  **skates**
   patines

6.  **picnic**
   picnic

7. **hamburger**
   hamburguesa

8. **hot dog**
   hot dog

9. **clouds**
   nubes

10.  **wind**
    viento

11. **lightning**
    relámpago

12. **thunderstorm**
    tormenta eléctrica

Windy fall

Otoño ventoso

1. **leaves**
   hojas

2. **rake**
   rastrillo

3. **pile**
   montón

4. **wheelbarrow**
   carretilla

5. **clippers**
   tijeras de podar

6. **broom**
   escoba

7. **bulbs**
tubérculos

8. **football**
fútbol americano

9. **soccer**
fútbol

10. **pumpkin**
calabaza

11. **woodpecker**
pájaro carpintero

12. **nuts**
nueces

Snowy winter

Invierno nevado

1.  **snow**
nieve

2. **snowflakes**
copos de nieve

3. **snowman**
muñeco de nieve

4. **snowball**
bola de nieve

5.  **icicles**
carámbanos

6. **sled**
trineo

7. **ice skating**
patinar sobre hielo

8. **skiing**
esquiar

9.  **hat**
sombrero

10.  **jacket**
chaqueta

11. **gloves**
guantes

12. **scarf**
bufanda

Up in the
night sky

Arriba en el cielo

1. 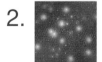 moon
luna

2. stars
estrellas

3. 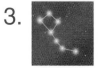 constellation
constelación

4. meteor
meteoro

5. comet
cometa

6. planets
planetas

7. **astronomer**
astrónomo

8. **telescope**
telescopio

9. **full moon**
luna llena

10. **half moon**
cuarto menguante

11. **crescent moon**
cuarto creciente

12. **new moon**
luna nueva

Out in space

En el espacio exterior

Saturn

Jupiter

Neptune

Uranus

Pluto

1. **The Sun**
Sol

2. **Mercury**
Mercurio

3. **Venus**
Venus

4. **Earth**
Tierra

5. **Mars**
Marte

6. **Jupiter**
Júpiter

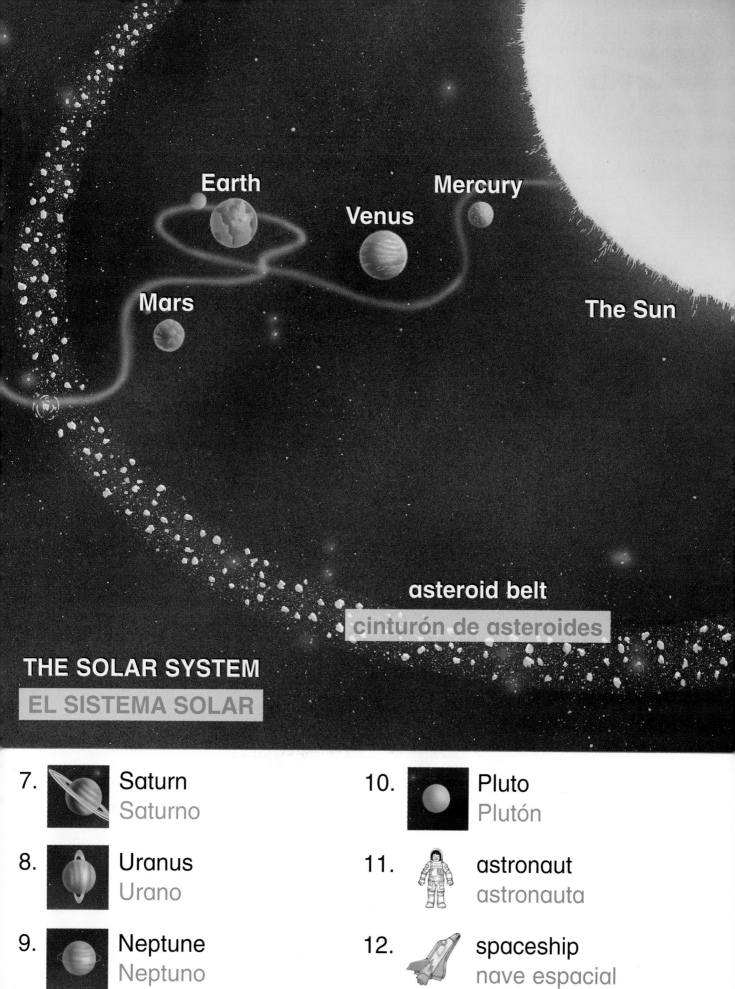

Earth

Mercury

Venus

Mars

The Sun

asteroid belt
cinturón de asteroides

THE SOLAR SYSTEM
EL SISTEMA SOLAR

7. Saturn
Saturno

8. Uranus
Urano

9. Neptune
Neptuno

10. Pluto
Plutón

11. astronaut
astronauta

12. spaceship
nave espacial

Appendix

Apéndice

The Alphabet El abecedario

A a B b C c

D d E e F f

G g H h I i

J j K k L l

M m N n O o

P p Q q R r

S s T t U u

V v W w X x

Y y Z z

Numbers Los numeros

1	one	●	uno
2	two	●●	dos
3	three	●●●	tres
4	four	●●●●	cuatro
5	five	●●●●●	cinco
6	six	●●●●●●	seis
7	seven	●●●●●●●	siete
8	eight	●●●●●●●●	ocho
9	nine	●●●●●●●●●	nueve
10	ten	●●●●●●●●●●	diez
11	eleven	●●●●●●●●●●●	once
12	twelve	●●●●●●●●●●●●	doce
13	thirteen	●●●●●●●●●●●●●	trece
14	fourteen	●●●●●●●●●●●●●●	catorce
15	fifteen	●●●●●●●●●●●●●●●	quince
16	sixteen	●●●●●●●●●●●●●●●●	dieciséis
17	seventeen	●●●●●●●●●●●●●●●●●	diecisiete
18	eighteen	●●●●●●●●●●●●●●●●●●	dieciocho
19	nineteen	●●●●●●●●●●●●●●●●●●●	diecinueve
20	twenty	●●●●●●●●●●●●●●●●●●●●	veinte

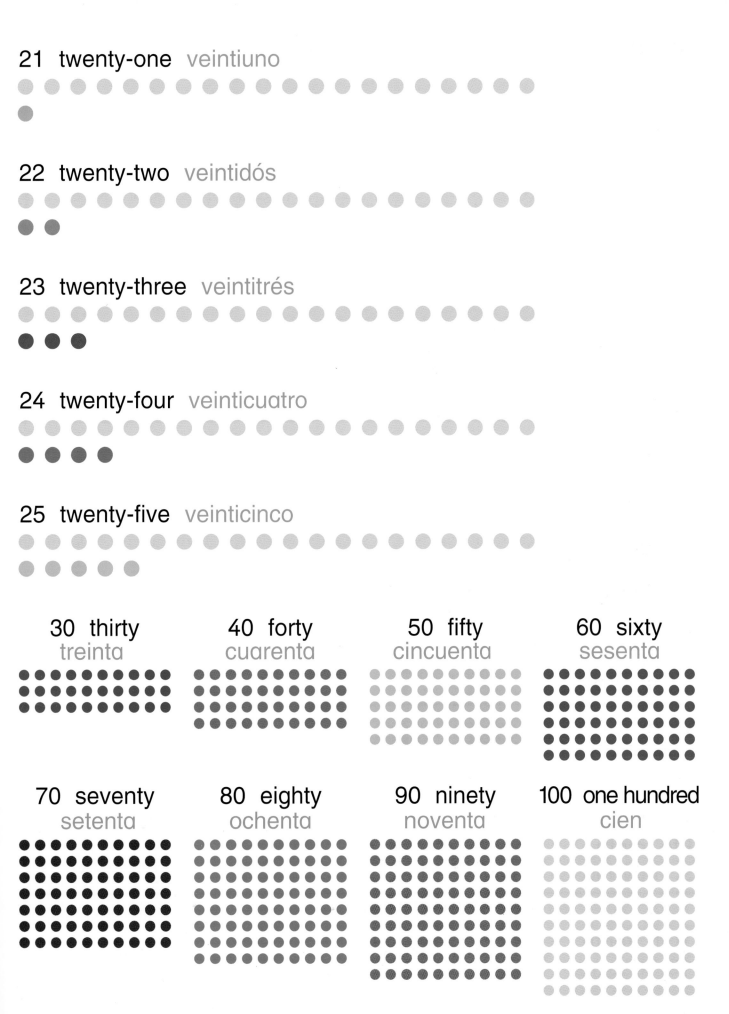

21 twenty-one veintiuno

22 twenty-two veintidós

23 twenty-three veintitrés

24 twenty-four veinticuatro

25 twenty-five veinticinco

30 thirty
treinta

40 forty
cuarenta

50 fifty
cincuenta

60 sixty
sesenta

70 seventy
setenta

80 eighty
ochenta

90 ninety
noventa

100 one hundred
cien

Ordinal Numbers Numeros ordinales

1st first
1.° primero

★ ☆ ☆ ☆ ☆ ☆ ☆ ☆ ☆ ☆

2nd second
2.° segundo

☆ ★ ☆ ☆ ☆ ☆ ☆ ☆ ☆ ☆

3rd third
3.° tercero

☆ ☆ ★ ☆ ☆ ☆ ☆ ☆ ☆ ☆

4th fourth
4.° cuarto

☆ ☆ ☆ ★ ☆ ☆ ☆ ☆ ☆ ☆

5th fifth
5.° quinto

☆ ☆ ☆ ☆ ★ ☆ ☆ ☆ ☆ ☆

6th sixth
6.° sexto

☆ ☆ ☆ ☆ ☆ ★ ☆ ☆ ☆ ☆

7th seventh
7.° séptimo

☆ ☆ ☆ ☆ ☆ ☆ ★ ☆ ☆ ☆

8th eighth
8.° octavo

☆ ☆ ☆ ☆ ☆ ☆ ☆ ★ ☆ ☆

9th ninth
9.° noveno

☆ ☆ ☆ ☆ ☆ ☆ ☆ ☆ ★ ☆

10th tenth
10.° décimo

☆ ☆ ☆ ☆ ☆ ☆ ☆ ☆ ☆ ★

Colors   Los colores

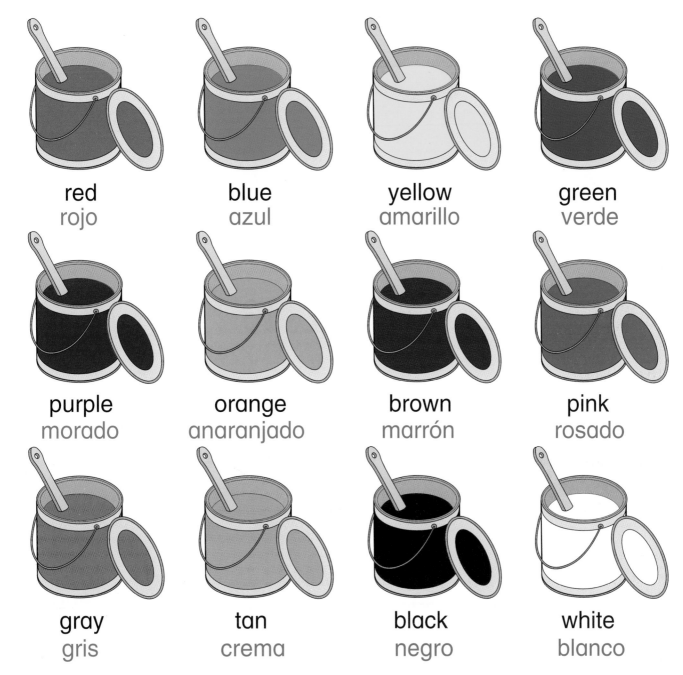

red
rojo

blue
azul

yellow
amarillo

green
verde

purple
morado

orange
anaranjado

brown
marrón

pink
rosado

gray
gris

tan
crema

black
negro

white
blanco

Shapes   Figuras geométricas

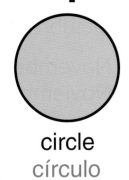

circle
círculo

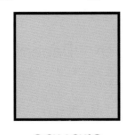

square
cuadrado

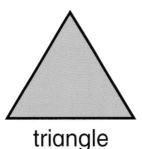

triangle
triángulo

rectangle
rectángulo

Days of the Week Los días de la semana

Sunday
Domingo

Monday
Lunes

Tuesday
Martes

Wednesday
Miércoles

Thursday
Jueves

Friday
Viernes

Saturday
Sábado

Sunday	Monday	Tuesday	Wednesday	Thursday	Friday	Saturday
		1	2	3	4	5
6	7	8	9	10	11	12
13	14	15	16	17	18	19

Months of the Year Los meses del año

January
Enero

February
Febrero

March
Marzo

April
Abril

May
Mayo

June
Junio

July
Julio

August
Agosto

September
Septiembre

October
Octubre

November
Noviembre

December
Diciembre

January
S	M	T	W	T	F	S
						1
2	3	4	5	6	7	8
9	10	11	12	13	14	15
16	17	18	19	20	21	22
23	24	25	26	27	28	29
30	31					

February
S	M	T	W	T	F	S
		1	2	3	4	5
6	7	8	9	10	11	12
13	14	15	16	17	18	19
20	21	22	23	24	25	26
27	28	29				

March
S	M	T	W	T	F	S
				1	2	3	4
5	6	7	8	9	10	11
12	13	14	15	16	17	18
19	20	21	22	23	24	25
26	27	28	29	30	31	

April
S	M	T	W	T	F	S
						1
2	3	4	5	6	7	8
9	10	11	12	13	14	15
16	17	18	19	20	21	22
23	24	25	26	27	28	29
30						

May
S	M	T	W	T	F	S
	1	2	3	4	5	6
7	8	9	10	11	12	13
14	15	16	17	18	19	20
21	22	23	24	25	26	27
28	29	30	31			

June
S	M	T	W	T	F	S
				1	2	3
4	5	6	7	8	9	10
11	12	13	14	15	16	17
18	19	20	21	22	23	24
25	26	27	28	29	30	

July
S	M	T	W	T	F	S
						1
2	3	4	5	6	7	8
9	10	11	12	13	14	15
16	17	18	19	20	21	22
23	24	25	26	27	28	29
30	31					

August
S	M	T	W	T	F	S
		1	2	3	4	5
6	7	8	9	10	11	12
13	14	15	16	17	18	19
20	21	22	23	24	25	26
27	28	29	30	31		

September
S	M	T	W	T	F	S
					1	2
3	4	5	6	7	8	9
10	11	12	13	14	15	16
17	18	19	20	21	22	23
24	25	26	27	28	29	30

October
S	M	T	W	T	F	S
1	2	3	4	5	6	7
8	9	10	11	12	13	14
15	16	17	18	19	20	21
22	23	24	25	26	27	28
29	30	31				

November
S	M	T	W	T	F	S
			1	2	3	4
5	6	7	8	9	10	11
12	13	14	15	16	17	18
19	20	21	22	23	24	25
26	27	28	29	30		

December
S	M	T	W	T	F	S
					1	2
3	4	5	6	7	8	9
10	11	12	13	14	15	16
17	18	19	20	21	22	23
24	25	26	27	28	29	30
31						

Time La hora

5:00

5 pm

five o'clock
cinco en punto

5:15

five fifteen
cinco y quince

a quarter past five
cinco y cuarto

5:30

five thirty
cinco y treinta

half past five
cinco y media

5:45

five forty-five
cinco y cuarenta y cinco

a quarter to six
seis menos cuarto

Words

Words shown in red are in illustrations only. Words in black are in illustrations and text.

smoke detector **73**
smokestack **66**
snack bar **62**
snail **85**
snakes **98**
sneakers **16**
sneeze **39**
snorkel **86**
snow **114**
snowball **114**
snowdrift **114-115**
snowflakes **114**
snowman **114**
snowplow **114-115**
soap **15**
soccer **113**
socks **16**
soda **63**
sofa **12**
soil **108**
Solar System **119**
sore throat **38**
soup **59**
South America **8**
space **118**
spaceship **119**
spider **92**
spine **29**
spoon **19**
sports store **43**
spots **103**
spout **86**
spray **51**
spring **106**
sprout **108**
spurs **94-95**
squirrel **107**
stand **21**
stars **116**
statue **68-69**
steel drum **68-69**
steering wheel **20-21**
Stegosaurus **97**
stem **109**
steps **69**
stereo **60**
stethoscope **50**
sting **92-93**
stir **79**
stockings **16-17**
stomach **28**
stomachache **38**
stones **84**
stop sign **20-21**
stores **42-43, 56-57**
stove **12**
stove **18-19**
straight **7**
straw **34-35**
street **10, 68**
street **42-43**
street cleaner **67**
stretch **32-33**
stretcher **52**
stripes **103**
student **22**
stuffed animal **16-17**
subway **67**
suit **16-17**

summer **110**
The Sun **118**
sun **108-109**
sunblock **82**
sunburn **82**
sunflowers **108-109**
sunglasses **82-83**
sunrise **90**
sunset **74**
sunshine **108**
supermarket **54**
surfboard **83**
surprised **30**
sushi **35**
swan **110-111**
sweater **16**
sweatshirt **17**
sweep **112-113**
swim **83**
swing **36**

T _____

T-shirt **17**
table **12**
tablecloth **78**
tablets **51**
taco **34**
tail **99**
talk **61**
tall **67**
taxi **42**
taxi **66-67**
tea **78-79**
teacher **22**
teapot **78-79**
teeth **6**
telephone **10**
telescope **117**
television **60**
temperature **38-39**
tennis **110**
tent **76-77**
tent **90**
tentacles **87**
theater **69**
thermometer **38**
thermometer **50-51**
think **27**
through **32**
throw **37**
thumb **28-29**
thunder **110-111**
thunderstorm **111**
ticks **93**
ticket **76**
ticket booth **62-63**
tide pool **84**
tie **16-17**
tiger **98**
tired **30**
tissues **38**
toaster **18-19**
toe **29**
toilet **15**
toilet paper **15**
tomato **58**
tongue depressors **38-39**
tooth **6**

toothbrush **14**
toothpaste **15**
top **42-43**
towel **15**
tower **24-25**
town **56**
toys **44**
toy store **43**
tractor **88**
traffic **42**
traffic light **42**
traffic light **10-11**
train **44**
trapeze **76**
tray **34**
tree **11**
triangle **41**
Triceratops **96**
trombone **40-41, 60-61**
trowel **106-107**
truck **42**
trumpet **40**
trunk **99**
tuba **40**
tugboat **75**
tumble **33**
turtle **46**
turtle **86-87**
tusk **98-99**
TV **12-13, 60-61**
twins **4-5**
Tyrannosaurus Rex **97**

U _____

umbrella **82-83**
umbrella **109**
uncle **5**
under **32, 86**
underground **108-109**
underwear **16**
United States **8-9, 80-81**
upside-down **36-37**
Uranus **119**
USA **80**
USA **8-9, 80-81**

V _____

vase **12-13, 60-61**
vegetables **54-55**
Venus **118**
videotape **49**
violin **40**
volcano **97**

W _____

waiter **79**
waiting room **51, 52**
walk **23**
walker **53**
warehouse **75**
warmups **32-33**
wash **13**
washcloth **14-15**
wastebasket **27**
watch **61**
water **14**
water (verb) **107**
water hole **102-103**
waterfall **90**

watering can **106-107**
waterskiing **110**
wave (noun) **82**
wave (verb) **74-75, 76-77**
wear **16**
web **92**
weigh **50-51**
wetlands **81**
whale **86**
wheel **4-5, 20-21**
wheelbarrow **112**
wheelchair **53**
wheelchair **4-5, 48-49, 106-107**
whistle **36-37, 82-83**
wichity grubs **100**
wind **111**
window **11**
wings **101**
winter **114**
wire **71**
wok **78-79**
woman **4-5**
wombat **101**
wood **70-71**
woodpecker **113**
woods **91**
world **8**
worried **31**
wrapping paper **64**
wrist **29**
write **27**

X _____

X ray **53**

y _____

yard **11**
yawn **31**

Z _____

zebra **102**
zoo **98**

Palabras

Las palabras en tinta roja están sólo en las ilustraciones. Las palabras en tinta negra están en las ilustraciones y en el texto.

Verbs

Topic 6: Good morning!
brush
cook
eat
get dressed
sleep
wash

Topic 10: Here comes the school bus!
lean
push
sit
stand

Topic 11: Time for school!
ride
walk

Topic 12: What are you making?
build
cut
listen
look
paint

Topic 13: Where's my homework?
draw
read
think
write

Topic 15: What's new in the hall?
cry
frown
laugh
smile
yawn

Topic 16: Gym time!
crawl
hop
jump
skip
tumble

Topic 18: Let's play!
bounce
catch
climb
fall
kick
run
throw

Topic 19: What's the matter?
cough
lie down
sneeze

Topic 20: Music!
beat
blow
clap
sing

Topic 24: Let's go to the library!
check out
return

Topic 30: Nice evening!
help
play
practice
rest
talk
watch

Topic 39: Great restaurant!
chop
pour
serve
stir

Topic 41: Beach day
dive
float
swim

Topic 44: Working on the farm
drive
feed
milk
pick

Subjects

Animals

Topic 23: Can we have a pet?
bird
cat
dog
fish
kitten
mouse
puppy
turtle

Topic 41: Beach day
seagull

Topic 42: We found a tide pool!
clams
crabs
duck
geese
goose
minnows
pelican
snail

Topic 43: What's under the sea?
dolphin
jellyfish
octopus
sea horse
shark
whale

Topic 44: Working on the farm
cow
hen
pig
rooster
sheep

Topic 45: Camping out
bear
deer
frog

Topic 46: Bugs!
ant
bee
butterfly
caterpillar
firefly
mosquito
spider
tick

Topic 47: Ranch in the desert
buffalo
coyote
horse
lizard

prairie dog
rattlesnake
scorpion

Topic 48: Dinosaur days
dinosaurs
Diplodocus
Oviraptor
Pterosaur
Stegosaurus
Triceratops
Tyrannosaurus Rex

Topic 49: Who lives in the zoo?
apes
elephant
lion
monkeys
peacock
snakes
tiger

Topic 50: I'm in Australia!
dingo
emu
joey
kangaroo
koala
kookaburra
parrot
wichity grubs
wombat

Topic 51: I'm in Africa!
baboon
chimpanzee
flamingo
gazelle
giraffe
gorilla
hippopotamus
leopard
zebra

Topic 52: I'm in Asia!
camel
cobra
crocodile
egret
orangutan
panda
rhinoceros

Topic 53: Spring is here!
rabbit
raccoon
robin
squirrel

Topic 56: Windy fall
woodpecker